AND DUBIOUS

ACHIEVEMENTS IN

FOOTBALL HISTORY

•

JOHN S. SNYDER

CHRONICLE BOOKS
SAN FRANCISCO

Printed in Singapore.

ISBN 0-8118-0280-9

Library of Congress Cataloging in Publication Data
available.

Design by TBH/Typecast, Inc.

Distributed in Canada by Raincoast Books,
112 East Third Avenue, Vancouver, B.C. V5T 1C8

10   9   8   7   6   5   4   3   2   1

Chronicle Books
275 Fifth Street
San Francisco, CA 94103

Introduction

A football is designed to sail in a perfect arc off the hand or the foot—or to bounce crazily and unpredictably along the ground. Football records have likewise sailed straight and bounced wildly. Predictably, stars like Joe Montana, Jim Brown, O. J. Simpson, and Jerry Rice have their prominent place in the record books, but records have also bounded unexpectedly into the hands of performers such as Timmy Smith and Percy Howard. And then there is the truly bizarre: Take Chester Marcol of the Green Bay Packers, who in 1980 took his own blocked field goal into the end zone for a touchdown and a 12–6 win over the Chicago Bears.

This book is a journey through time, not only honoring those who have established records but also bringing their feats to life by capturing the stories behind the numbers. Collected here are famous, forgotten, and untold tales of the many men who have fumbled, tackled, passed, and blocked their way into the record books. After more than a century of football, each of these athletes is still *the only player* to achieve his extraordinary feat.

The first three quarters of this book give playing time to professional football, the final quarter to college teams. In all, more than 200 exploits are recounted.

The professional records that follow are from the National Football League, which began play in 1920, and the American Football League, which was in existence from 1960 through 1969 and was absorbed into the NFL in the merger of 1970. The NFL did not begin to compute individual statistics until 1932, however, so there may be a few records set in the early years that are unofficial or "lost" in time.

College football began play in 1869, but meticulous records were not kept until 1937. Unless otherwise noted, the records in this book are post-1937 and cover only what is now considered NCAA Division 1-A, or "major college." Although many of the schools mentioned in this book are no longer 1-A, and a few have even given up the sport entirely, all were considered major college at the time the record was established.

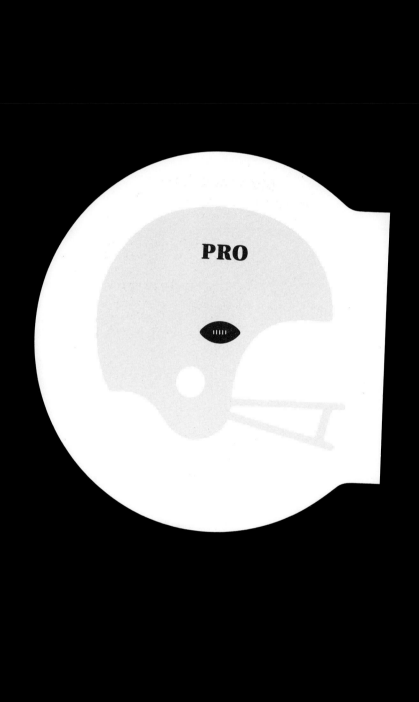

Marcus Allen

THE ONLY PLAYER to score on a 74-yard run in a Super Bowl.

Marcus Allen accounted for the longest run in Super Bowl history, on January 22, 1984, in the Los Angeles Raiders 38–9 win over the Washington Redskins in Tampa. From his own 26-yard line, Allen started left, then retraced his steps and burst up the middle and outraced the Washington defense to the end zone.

Alan Ameche

THE ONLY PLAYER to rush for more than 190 yards in his first NFL game.

Alan Ameche won the Heisman Trophy as a fullback at the University of Wisconsin in 1954, and a year later came to the Baltimore Colts as a first-round draft choice. In his first carry in the NFL, on September 25, 1955, Ameche galloped 79 yards for a touchdown. In all, he gained 194 yards on 21 carries as the Colts defeated the Chicago Bears 23–17 in Baltimore. Ameche is also the only player to score in overtime in an NFL championship game. On December 28, 1958, his one-yard plunge gave the Colts a 23–17 win and a championship over the New York Giants at Yankee Stadium.

Ken Anderson

THE ONLY NFL player to complete
20 consecutive passes in a single game.

Ken Anderson was nearly perfect for the
Cincinnati Bengals on January 2, 1983,
against the Houston Oilers at the Astrodome. He connected on 27 of 31 passes,
including 20 in a row between the first and
third quarters in a 35–27 win. Anderson
also holds the record for highest completion percentage in a game (minimum 20
attempts), which he set on November 10,
1974, against the Steelers, when he completed 20 of 22 in a 17–10 victory. Anderson's completion percentage of 70.55 in
1982 is the best ever for a season.

Willie "Flipper" Anderson

THE ONLY NFL player to gain 336 yards in pass receptions in one game.

Entering the game on November 26, 1989, Willie Anderson had never gained more more than 112 yards receiving in a game, and certainly did not seem to be a candidate to break Stephone Paige's NFL record of 309. Anderson stunningly surpassed that mark with 15 receptions and 336 yards, leading the Los Angeles Rams from a 17–3 fourth-quarter deficit to beat the Saints 20–17 in overtime in New Orleans.

Elmer Angsman

THE ONLY PLAYER to run for two 70-yard touchdowns in an NFL championship game.

In the 1947 NFL championship matchup between the Philadelphia Eagles and Chicago Cardinals at Comiskey Park, the star runner was supposed to be Philadelphia's Steve Van Buren, who became the first 1,000-yard rusher in the league in 13 years. Van Buren was held to 26 yards in 18 carries, however, and it was Chicago's Elmer Angsman who stole the show. Angsman scored on a pair of 70-yard runs up the middle of the Eagle defense in the second and fourth quarters to give Chicago a 28–21 victory.

Jim Bakken

THE ONLY PLAYER to attempt nine field goals in a game.

The St. Louis Cardinal offense bogged down often enough on September 24, 1967, to allow Jim Bakken to try for three points nine times against the Steelers at Pitt Stadium in Pittsburgh. Bakken missed twice, but hit from 18, 24, 33, 29, 24, 32, and 23 yards to lead the Cardinals to a 28–14 win.

Sammy Baugh

THE ONLY PLAYER to throw four touchdown passes and intercept four passes in the same game.

Playing in an era when nearly everyone played both offense and defense, Sammy Baugh was the best of them all in a career that lasted from 1937 to 1952, all with the Washington Redskins. On November 14, 1943, he threw four TD passes and intercepted four Detroit Lion passes in a 42–20 win in Washington. In that year's campaign, Baugh led the NFL in passing, interceptions, and punting. He holds the record for highest punting average in a season (51.4 yards in 1940) and in a career (45.1).

Steve Belichick

THE ONLY PLAYER whose lone NFL punt return went for 77 yards and a touchdown.

Steve Belichick was a fullback and linebacker for the Detroit Lions as a rookie in 1941. He fielded only one punt, which went for 77 yards and a touchdown in a 24–7 loss to the Green Bay Packers. After the season, Belichick entered the military and never returned to pro ball.

Bert Bell

THE ONLY NFL coach whose club completed fewer than 24 percent of its passes during a season.

Bert Bell's 1936 Philadelphia Eagles had undoubtedly the worst passing attack in pro football history. Eight different players combined to complete just 22.9 percent with 39 completions in 170 attempts. They also threw 35 interceptions and only three touchdown passes. The Eagles scored only 51 points all year and finished with a 1-11 record.

Hugo Bezdek

THE ONLY INDIVIDUAL to manage a major league baseball team and serve as head coach in the NFL.

Born in Prague, Czechoslovakia, Hugo Bezdek had a 166-187 record as skipper of the Pittsburgh Pirates from 1917 through 1919. He later coached college football at Arkansas, Oregon, and Penn State, and in 1937 accepted a position as head coach for the NFL's newest team, the Cleveland Rams. Bezdek had a miserable 1-13 record in two seasons with the Rams. Although he is the only individual to manage in the majors and coach pro football, he never played either sport at the major league level.

George Blanda

THE ONLY PRO player to score over 2,000 points in a career.

In 26 seasons and 340 games, both also records, George Blanda totaled 2,002 points on 9 touchdowns, 943 PATs, and 335 field goals with the Bears, Colts, Oilers, and Raiders between 1949 and 1975. He also threw for 236 touchdown passes as a quarterback, including 36 for Houston in 1961, third highest in history. Blanda reached cult status in 1970, when he helped lead the Raiders to four victories and a tie over a five-week period by coming off the bench as a field goal kicker and substitute quarterback with a series of remarkable last-minute heroics at the tender age of 43.

Cloyce Box

THE ONLY PLAYER to gain more than 300 yards receiving and catch four touchdown passes in the same game.

Cloyce Box ran the Baltimore Colts secondary dizzy on December 3, 1950, with 12 receptions for 302 yards and four touchdowns to lead the Detroit Lions to a 45–21 win at Baltimore. Three of the TDs came from the arm of Bobby Layne, the other from Fred Emke.

Jim Breech

THE ONLY PLAYER to score a point in 181 consecutive games.

In a streak still active at the beginning of the 1992 NFL season, Jim Breech scored either a point after touchdown, a field goal, or both in 181 straight games while kicking for the Oakland Raiders in 1979 and the Cincinnati Bengals since 1980.

Jim Brown

THE ONLY NFL player to score 126 touchdowns in a career.

Walter Payton broke most of Jim Brown's rushing records, but "Sweetness" fell one shy of Brown's mark for touchdowns in a career. With the Cleveland Browns from 1957 through 1965, Brown scored 106 times on the ground and on 20 occasions through pass receptions. Brown also holds records for most seasons leading the league in rushing with eight (no one else has more than four), including five in a row, and is the all-time leader in average gain per rushing attempt with 5.22 yards a carry.

Paul Brown

THE ONLY INDIVIDUAL to coach in the NFL championship game six years in a row.

The All-American Football Conference lasted four seasons beginning in 1946, and the Paul Brown–coached Cleveland Browns won the championship all four seasons, rolling to a 47-4-3 regular season record. The Browns were one of three AAFC teams absorbed into the NFL in 1950, and quickly dominated the league. They won the Eastern Conference six years in a row to reach the NFL title game, and took the league championship in 1950, 1954, and 1955.

Timmy Brown

THE ONLY PLAYER to run two kick-offs of 90 yards or longer for touch-downs in the same game.

In a strange game between Timmy Brown's Eagles and the Dallas Cowboys on November 6, 1966, at Franklin Field in Philadelphia, Brown ran back kickoffs 93 and 90 yards for scores. Both came in the first half, and thanks to Brown's TD dashes and teammate Aaron Martin's 67-yard punt return, the Eagles had a 24–17 half-time lead despite gaining only six yards from scrimmage. Philadelphia held on for a 24–23 victory.

Tom Brown

THE ONLY ATHLETE to play major league baseball and appear as a player in the Super Bowl.

Tom Brown was drafted in the second round in 1963 by the Green Bay Packers as a defensive back from Maryland, but tried his hand at baseball first. In 61 games with the Washington Senators in 1963, Brown batted .147 in 116 at bats as a first baseman–outfielder. That experience led him back to football, and Brown was soon Green Bay's starting safety. He played in the first two Super Bowls following the 1966 and 1967 seasons.

Adrian Burk

THE ONLY PLAYER to throw seven touchdown passes but gain fewer than 400 yards in a game.

Adrian Burk is one of five quarterbacks in NFL history to throw seven touchdown passes in a single game and the only one to accomplish the feat with less than 400 yards passing. He was very economical, with 19 completions on 27 attempts for 227 yards in leading the Philadelphia Eagles to a 49–21 win over the Redskins in Washington on October 17, 1954. Burk, also the Eagles punter, pinned the Redskins deep in their own territory with three kicks inside the 10-yard line.

Billy Cannon

THE ONLY PRO player to gain 330 yards from scrimmage in a game.

Billy Cannon ripped apart the New York Titans defense on December 10, 1961, with 216 yards rushing and 114 receiving, scoring five touchdowns in the Houston Oilers 48–21 win at the Polo Grounds. He reached the end zone on runs of 61, 53, and 2 yards, and on passes from George Blanda of 67 and 15 yards.

Gino Cappelletti

THE ONLY PRO player to score four two-point conversions in his career.

The two-point conversion was an option in pro football only with the American Football League from 1960 to 1969. Gino Cappelletti scored four of them in his career, all with the Boston Patriots from 1960 through 1970, along with 42 touchdowns, 176 field goals, and 346 conventional one-point conversions.

Jack Christiansen

THE ONLY PLAYER to return two punts in a game for touchdowns twice in a career.

In only six instances in NFL history has a player returned two punts in a game for touchdowns, and Jack Christiansen has accounted for two of them, both as a rookie with the Detroit Lions in 1951. The first was on October 14 in a 27–21 loss to the Los Angeles Rams in Detroit, the second in a 52–35 win over the Green Bay Packers on November 22, 1951, again in the Motor City. Christiansen also holds NFL records for most punt returns for touchdowns in a season with four, and in a career with eight.

Algy Clark

THE ONLY COACH whose final NFL game was a 64–0 loss.

Algy Clark coached eight games in the NFL, all with the Cincinnati Reds in 1934, and he lost every one of them while being outscored 243–10. The finale was the worst regular season defeat in league history. Cincinnati was to have played the Eagles in Philadelphia on Sunday, November 4, at Baker Bowl, but because of rain and low advance ticket sales, the game was moved to Tuesday night, November 6, at Temple Stadium. On Monday night, the Reds found out the team had been sold and the final three games would be played by a semipro club. The disheartened Reds then went out and lost 64–0 to the Eagles.

Potsy Clark

THE ONLY COACH to lead his club
to seven consecutive shutout victories.

Radio station owner George Richards
purchased the Portsmouth Spartans of the
NFL, where Potsy Clark had coached since
1930, for $15,000 on June 30, 1934. He
then moved them to Detroit, where they
were renamed the Lions. The new club
stunned the league by shutting out their
opponents through the first seven games of
the season. In fact, no one was able to pen-
etrate the Detroit 20-yard line. The streak
was broken in the eighth game, but the
Lions won anyway 40–7, piling up an NFL
record 426 yards rushing. Detroit won its
first 10 games, but dropped the last 3, including the first of the now traditional
Thanksgiving Day games.

Wayne Clark

THE ONLY NFL quarterback to throw 14 career interceptions without a touchdown.

Wayne Clark holds the dubious pro football record for most interceptions without a single career TD pass. He played for the San Diego Chargers, Cincinnati Bengals, and Kansas City Chiefs between 1970 and 1975 and threw 120 passes, completing only 43 percent.

Gary Collins

THE ONLY PLAYER to catch three touchdown passes in an NFL championship game.

Gary Collins caught three TD passes from Frank Ryan in the NFL championship game on December 27, 1964, to lead the Browns to a 27–0 stunning upset victory over the heavily favored Baltimore Colts in Cleveland. Collins's scoring grabs covered 18, 42, and 51 yards. He also had five receptions for 130 yards.

Charlie Conerly

THE ONLY ROOKIE quarterback to throw 22 touchdown passes.

Few NFL quarterbacks make an impact as a rookie, but Charlie Conerly was an exception with the New York Giants in 1948 as he tossed 22 touchdown passes, 10 to another rookie named Bill Swiacki. The 1948 Giants were a bad team, finishing with a 4-8 record, but in 14 seasons in New York, Conerly played in four NFL championship games. He finished his career in 1961 with 173 touchdown passes, which at the time was second best in the NFL behind only Sammy Baugh.

Jimmy Conzelman

THE ONLY NFL coach to avoid defeat despite his club gaining only 14 yards in offense.

Jimmy Conzelman's Chicago Cardinals gained only 14 yards in offense, but struggled to a 0–0 tie against the Detroit Lions on September 15, 1940, because the defense allowed only 16 yards. The 30 yards in offense by the two teams is the lowest in the NFL history by a wide margin. The next lowest figure is 136. The Cardinals had moved the game to Buffalo due to small crowds in Chicago. A terrific thunderstorm hit with the opening kickoff and continued throughout the game. According to the Associated Press dispatch, the game "had more the flavor of water polo."

Frank Corral

THE ONLY PLAYER to score for every point in a NFL postseason game.

In the NFC championship game on January 6, 1980, Frank Corral accounted for all of the points by kicking field goals of 19, 21, and 23 yards as the Los Angeles Rams defeated the Buccaneers 9–0 in Tampa.

Roger Craig

THE ONLY NFL player to gain over 1,000 yards rushing and receiving in the same season.

Roger Craig was an all-purpose star for the San Francisco 49ers in 1985. He rushed 214 times for 1,050 yards and gained an additional 1,016 yards on 92 receptions. Craig scored nine times on the ground and six through the air.

Don Currivan

THE ONLY NFL player with at least
75 career receptions with an average of
over 25 yards per catch.

Don Currivan played in the NFL from
1943 through 1949 with the Chicago Cardinals, Boston Yanks, and Los Angeles
Rams, and caught 78 career passes for
1,979 yards, an average of 25.4 yards per
reception, and 24 touchdowns. In 1947
with Boston, despite playing with a quarterback named Boley Dancewicz who completed only 39 percent of his passes, Currivan caught 24 for 782 yards and 9 TDs,
for an average of 32.6 yards.

Tommy Davis

THE ONLY NFL player to connect on
234 points after touchdowns.

The point after is almost automatic, but
Tommy Davis was more automatic than
anyone else. The 234 consecutive PATs
came on the first 234 attempts of his pro
career, beginning in 1959 and ending in
1965, all with the San Francisco 49ers.
When he finally missed one, on December
12, 1965, it was hardly noticed, as the
49ers lost to the Chicago Bears 61–20
while Gayle Sayers was running wild with
six touchdowns. Davis finished his career
with 348 PATs in 350 attempts, and his
punting average of 44.7 yards is the NFL's
second best career mark.

Dudley DeGroot

THE ONLY COACH to lose an NFL championship game because of a safety.

Dudley DeGroot's Washington Redskins played in the 1945 NFL championship on December 16 against the Cleveland Rams. With the score 0–0 in the first period, Washington's Sammy Baugh dropped back into his own end zone to let fly with a pass, when a strong gust of wind from Lake Erie blew across Municipal Stadium and steered the ball into the goalpost. Under the rules then in effect, the play was ruled a safety, and the Rams had a 2–0 lead. That proved to be the margin of victory, as the Rams won 15–14.

Tom Dempsey

THE ONLY PRO to kick a 63-yard field goal.

Tom Dempsey overcame the handicap of being born with half of his right foot and the stub of a right hand to become a defensive end in high school and college and enjoy an 11-year career as a placekicker in the NFL. His record 63-yard field goal could not have come at a more dramatic moment. On November 8, 1970, the Saints were trailing the heavily favored Detroit Lions 17–16 in New Orleans with time on the clock for only one more play. Saints coach J. D. Roberts sent Dempsey in to try for three points from 63 yards. He booted the ball through the uprights to give New Orleans a 19–17 victory, one of only two games the Saints won all year.

Dan Devine

THE ONLY COACH to suffer a frac-
tured leg in his first NFL game.

After a fine career at the University of
Missouri, Dan Devine became coach of the
Green Bay Packers in 1971. In his debut
on September 19 against the New York Giants in Green Bay, Devine got entangled in
a sideline pileup and came out of it with a
broken leg. To make matters worse, the
Packers lost 42–40. The game also featured
a missed field goal returned 100 yards for a
touchdown by Green Bay's Ken Ellis, two
Giants touchdowns scored within six seconds when the Packers' Dave Hampton
twice fumbled into the end zone, and four
Fran Tarkenton touchdown passes.

Eric Dickerson

THE ONLY NFL player to rush for
more than 2,100 yards in a season.

With the Los Angeles Rams in 1984, Eric
Dickerson ran the ball 379 times for 2,105
yards and 14 touchdowns to break the
rushing mark of 2,003 yards set by O. J.
Simpson in 1973.

Aldo "Buff" Donelli

THE ONLY INDIVIDUAL to coach in the NFL and at the collegiate level at the same time.

Aldo Donelli was coach at the highly successful Duquense University program, when two games into the Pittsburgh Steelers 1941 season, owner Art Rooney asked Donelli to coach the two clubs simultaneously. The experiment lasted five weeks, all of which were Steeler losses, when NFL commissioner Elmer Layden told Donelli to choose one job or the other. Donelli wisely selected undefeated Duquense. The college outfit finished 8-0 and was ranked eighth in the final Associated Press poll.

Tony Dorsett

THE ONLY PLAYER to gain 99 yards rushing on one play.

Tony Dorsett accounted for the only 99-yard running play in NFL history on January 3, 1983, for the Dallas Cowboys against the Minnesota Vikings at the Metrodome. It broke the mark of 97 yards set by Andy Uram (Green Bay Packers, 1939) and Bob Gage (Pittsburgh Steelers, 1949). The Cowboys were backed up on their own one-yard line because of a fumbled kickoff return, when Dorsett skirted the right end and outran the Minnesota defense to the end zone. The Cowboys were trailing 24–13 at the time and eventually went ahead 27–24, but lost the game 31–27.

Bobby Douglass

THE ONLY NFL quarterback to rush for 968 yards in a season.

Bobby Douglass set the all-time NFL record for most rushing yards by a quarterback in a season with the 1972 Chicago Bears with 968 yards on 141 carries, an average of 6.9 yards an attempt, and eight touchdowns. The Bears finished the year 4-9-1 despite leading the league in rushing, because they were also last in passing. The team averaged fewer than 15 passing attempts per game and completed only 38 percent of those.

Chuck Dressen

THE ONLY INDIVIDUAL to manage a
major league baseball club and play in
the National Football League.

Chuck Dressen played for his hometown
Decatur (Illinois) Staleys, a forerunner of
the Chicago Bears, with George Halas in
1920 and with Racine, Wisconsin, in 1922
and 1923. He played major league baseball
as a third baseman from 1925 to 1933,
mostly with the Cincinnati Reds. He was
manager of the Reds from 1934 through
1937, the Brooklyn Dodgers from 1951
through 1953, the Washington Senators
from 1955 to 1957, the Milwaukee Braves
in 1960 and 1961, and the Detroit Tigers
from 1963 until his death in 1966.

Fred Dryer

THE ONLY PLAYER to be credited for two safeties in one game.

The record for safeties in a career is four, and the mark for a season is two, so Fred Dryer not only matched the record for a season in one game, but did it in one quarter on successive drives. Furthermore, those were the only two safeties Dryer recorded in his 13-year NFL career. On October 21, 1973, playing defensive end for the Los Angeles Rams, Dryer sacked Green Bay Packer quarterback Scott Hunter in the end zone. Dryer then dumped Hunter's replacement, Jim Del Gaizo, for another safety as the Rams rolled to a 24–7 win. After his playing career was over, Dryer starred in the title role in the long-running TV series "Hunter."

Sam Etcheverry

THE ONLY PLAYER to fumble six times in his NFL debut.

After a nine-year career in the Canadian Football League, Sam Etcheverry made his NFL debut as a quarterback for the St. Louis Cardinals on September 17, 1961. The bad news was that he fumbled six times. The good news was that he recovered four of them, and the Cardinals upset the New York Giants 21–10 at Yankee Stadium.

Fred "Dippy" Evans

THE ONLY PLAYER in NFL history to return two fumbles for touchdowns in a game.

Fred Evans played only part of one season in the NFL, but put himself in the record books when he picked up two fumbles from his defensive back position and ran for touchdowns. Playing for the Chicago Bears against the Washington Redskins at Wrigley Field on November 28, 1948, Evans took the fumbles 15 and 17 yards as Chicago ran up a 41–7 halftime lead on the way to a 48–13 victory.

Weeb Ewbank

THE ONLY COACH to win championships in the NFL and AFL.

Weeb Ewbank took over a moribund Baltimore Colts franchise as coach in 1954 and won National Football League championships in both 1958 and 1959. After the 1962 season, however, he was let go by Colt ownership and replaced by 33-year-old Don Shula. Less than four months later, Ewbank was named coach of the New York Jets of the upstart American Football League. By 1968, he had won the AFL title and met Shula and the Colts in Super Bowl III. Backed by quarterback Joe Namath's brash guarantee of victory, the Jets pulled off one of the biggest upsets of all time with a score of 16–7.

Tom Fears

THE ONLY PLAYER to catch 18 passes in an NFL game.

Entering the final game of the season on December 3, 1950, the Los Angeles Rams needed a victory over the Green Bay Packers to assure themselves of a playoff. Led by 18 receptions by Tom Fears from quarterbacks Norm Van Brocklin and Bob Waterfield, the Rams thrashed the Packers 54–14. Fears gained 189 yards and caught 10 passes in the fourth quarter.

Beattie Feathers

THE ONLY NFL player to rush for over 1,000 yards and average more than 7 yards per carry in the same season.

As a rookie from Tennessee in 1934, Beattie Feathers rushed for 1,004 yards for the Chicago Bears on just 101 carries for an incredible 9.94 yards per carry. The second best total by any other 1,000-yard rusher is Jim Brown's 6.40 in 1963. Behind the blocking of fullback Bronko Nagurski, Feathers scored eight touchdowns from his halfback position as the Bears rolled to a 13-0 record. Feathers was never again able to come close to his successful rookie campaign, however. For the remainder of his career, which lasted until 1940, he ran 259 times for 975 yards, or 3.76 yards a rush.

Frank Filchock

THE ONLY INDIVIDUAL to coach a professional football team wearing brown-and-gold uniforms with vertically striped socks.

Frank Filchock's Denver Broncos debuted in 1960, and for two seasons displayed without argument the worst uniforms in the history of professional sport. They wore brown helmets and brown pants with white shirts bearing brown numbers on the road and gold shirts with brown numbers at home. The uniforms were topped off, or bottomed off, with hideous brown-and-white vertically striped socks. In 1962, the uniforms were burned in a public ceremony, and the team colors were changed to orange and blue.

Ray Flaherty

THE ONLY COACH to lose an NFL championship game by the score of 73–0.

The highest score by one club in an NFL game and the largest margin of victory occurred in the 1940 championship game as the Chicago Bears stunned Ray Flaherty's Redskins 73–0 in Washington. Chicago scored 11 touchdowns, 7 in the second half, by 10 different players. Going into the game, however, the Redskins were 9-2, the Bears 8-3. Washington had not allowed more than 21 points to an opponent in any game all year, but Chicago matched that in the first quarter. Two years later, Flaherty and his club had their revenge. The final score in the 1942 NFL championship game was Washington 14, Chicago 6.

Joe Gibbs

THE ONLY COACH whose club scored 35 points in one quarter in a postseason game.

In Super Bowl XXII on January 31, 1988, Joe Gibbs's Washington Redskins trailed the Denver Broncos 10–0 after one period, then unleashed a terrible onslaught on the Orange Crush defense. The Redskins scored 35 unanswered points to take a 35-10 halftime lead. Quarterback Doug Williams threw four touchdown passes, including two, of 80 and 50 yards, to Ricky Sanders, and also tossed passes into the end zone of 27 yards to Gary Clark and 8 yards to Clint Didier. Timmy Smith also tallied on a 58-yard TD run.

Frank Gifford

THE ONLY PRO player to rush, receive, and pass for more than 10 touchdowns in his career.

Frank Gifford's versatility was always evident in his career with the New York Giants from 1952 through 1964. He rushed for 34 touchdowns, caught 43 more, and, in just 63 pass attempts off the halfback option, threw for 14 touchdown strikes.

Cookie Gilchrist

THE ONLY PRO player to combine for over 200 yards rushing and five rushing touchdowns in the same game.

With the Buffalo Bills on December 8, 1963, Cookie Gilchrist scored on runs of 4, 1, 1, 19, and 4 yards in crushing the New York Jets 45–14 at War Memorial Stadium. In all, he gained 243 yards on 36 carries.

Vencie Glenn

THE ONLY NFL player to return an interception 103 yards.

With the San Diego Chargers on November 29, 1987, Vencie Glenn picked off a John Elway pass three yards deep in the end zone and ran 103 yards for six points. The Chargers did little else to stop Elway and the Denver Broncos all day, however, as San Diego lost 31–17.

Otto Graham

THE ONLY PLAYER to throw three TD passes and score three TDs in an NFL postseason game.

Playing quarterback for the Cleveland Browns in the NFL championship game against the Detroit Lions in Cleveland on December 26, 1954, Otto Graham was a one-man show. He scored on three one-yard quarterback sneaks and tossed TD passes of 35 and 31 yards to Ray Renfro and eight yards to Darrell Brewster. The Browns won handily, 56–10.

Bud Grant

THE ONLY INDIVIDUAL to play in the NBA finals and coach in a Super Bowl.

Bud Grant was a six-foot, three-inch reserve forward on the 1949–50 NBA champion Minneapolis Lakers and coached the Minnesota Vikings in four Super Bowls following the 1969, 1973, 1974, and 1976 seasons. Unfortunately, the championship he earned in basketball eluded him in football. Grant is the only coach to lose four Super Bowls.

George Halas

THE ONLY INDIVIDUAL to coach for 40 seasons in the National Football League.

Oddly, George Halas's stint, all with the Chicago Bears, which he owned, was broken up into four 10-year segments. He was on the sidelines from 1920 through 1929, 1933 to 1942, 1946 through 1955, and 1958 until 1967. Halas chose to retire from coaching after the 1929, 1955, and 1967 seasons, and joined the Navy midway through the 1942 campaign. His career coaching record was 325 wins, 151 losses, and 31 ties.

Jim Hardy

THE ONLY NFL quarterback to
throw eight interceptions in a game.

Jim Hardy had a nightmare of a game
with the Chicago Cardinals on September
24, 1950, when he threw eight interceptions and lost two fumbles to the Philadelphia Eagles in a 45–7 defeat. Hardy completed only 12 of 39. But Hardy turned in
an incredible performance the following
week. On October 2 in Chicago, he threw
six touchdown passes, five to Bob Shaw,
who set a record for most touchdown receptions in a game (since tied). The Cardinals won 55–13.

Jim Hart

THE ONLY PLAYER to throw for a 98-yard completion without scoring a touchdown.

On December 10, 1972, Jim Hart and the St. Louis Cardinals were backed up on their one-yard line after a stand at the goal line which stopped the Los Angeles Rams on fourth down. Hart then dropped back into his own end zone and fired long to Bobby Moore (who less than a year later changed his name to Ahmad Rashad). Moore made a leaping catch at the Cardinal 40 and sped for pay dirt. Rams defensive back Al Clark pulled Moore down one yard shy of six points to end the unusual 98-yard play. Donny Anderson smashed over for a one-yard TD on the next play, as St. Louis triumphed 24–14.

Mack Herron

THE ONLY NFL player with over 400 yards rushing, receiving, and on punt and kickoff returns in a season.

With the New England Patriots in 1974, Mack Herron led the club in all four categories with 824 yards rushing, 474 receiving, 517 on punt returns, and 629 on kickoff returns. He scored 12 touchdowns.

Paul Hornung

THE ONLY NFL player to score 176 points in a season.

The multipurpose back set the record in 1960 with the Green Bay Packers when the schedule called for only 12 games. Hornung scored 13 touchdowns rushing, caught two passes for scores, kicked 41 PATs in 41 attempts, and connected on 15 field goals. He also threw two TD passes on halfback option plays.

Ken Houston

THE ONLY PLAYER to return nine
pass interceptions for touchdowns in a
career.

Playing from 1967 through 1980 with
the Houston Oilers and Washington Redskins, Ken Houston haunted opposing
quarterbacks by picking off 49 passes and
returning 9 for scores. His touchdown
mark broke the old record of seven held
jointly by Herb Adderley, Erich Barnes, and
Lem Barney. Houston returned four interceptions for scores in 1971, including two
in a game on December 19 in the Oilers'
49–33 win over the Chargers.

Percy Howard

THE ONLY PLAYER to catch a touchdown pass in a Super Bowl without catching a pass during the regular season.

Percy Howard, a rookie with the Dallas Cowboys in 1975, played in eight regular season games and two postseason contests as a wide receiver without catching a single pass. He did catch one pass during Super Bowl X, on January 18, 1976, against the Pittsburgh Steelers. The 34-yard reception for a touchdown was thrown by Roger Staubach with 1:56 remaining in the game, though the Cowboys lost 21–17. Due to injuries, Howard never played in another NFL game.

Chuck Howley

THE ONLY MEMBER of a losing team to be elected MVP in a Super Bowl.

Chuck Howley played at linebacker for the Dallas Cowboys in Super Bowl V on January 17, 1971, and intercepted two Baltimore Colts passes to earn Most Valuable Player honors. It was a hollow victory, however, as Dallas lost 16–13.

Don Hultz

THE ONLY PLAYER to recover nine opponents' fumbles in a season.

A rookie free-agent defensive end with the Minnesota Vikings in 1963, Don Hultz came up with one of football's fluke records. His nine fumble recoveries earned him the nickname "The Human Magnet," as balls literally fell into his hands game after game. Hultz stayed in the NFL until 1974 and also played for the Philadelphia Eagles and Chicago Bears, but recovered only three more fumbles in the succeeding 11 years.

Don Hutson

THE ONLY NFL player to score 29 points in one quarter.

In the second quarter on October 7, 1945, Don Hutson scored four touchdowns and kicked 5 extra points for 29 points to lead the Green Bay Packers past the Detroit Lions 57–21 in Milwaukee. The TDs all came on pass receptions from Irv Comp and Don McKay. In an 11-year career, from 1935 to 1945, Hutson led the NFL in receptions eight times, in scoring five seasons, and in interceptions once. He hauled in 99 touchdown passes, a record that stood until it was broken by Steve Largent in 1989.

Lindy Infante

THE ONLY COACH to win four
games by one point in a season.

The Green Bay Packers thrilled fans in
1989 with a series of stirring comeback victories. Lindy Infante and his staff helped
engineer four one-point victories by scores
of 35–34 against New Orleans, 14–13 over
Chicago, 20–19 versus Minnesota, and
17–16 against Tampa Bay. The Packers
also beat the Atlanta Falcons 23–21, Detroit 23–20 in overtime, and San Francisco
21–17. Green Bay finished the year with a
10-6 record.

LeRoy Irvin

THE ONLY NFL player to run back two punts of 75 yards or more for touchdowns in the same game.

LeRoy Irvin opened the scoring for the Los Angeles Rams on October 11, 1981, by running back an Atlanta Falcon punt 75 yards to give his club a 7–0 lead. The Rams pushed ahead 13–0 in the first quarter, but had fallen behind and trailed 35–27 with 8:23 left in the game when it was time for Irvin to go to work again. He took another punt at his own 16-yard line and streaked 84 yards for pay dirt to pull Los Angeles within a point. Frank Corral won it for the Rams 37–35 with a field goal with 24 seconds remaining.

Pop Ivy

THE ONLY PRO coach whose club scored 49 points and lost.

The early years of the American Football League were known for high scores, but none was better than the game on December 22, 1963, between Pop Ivy's Houston Oilers and the Raiders in Oakland. Houston led 21–7, 28–21, 35–28, and 49–42 before succumbing 52–49 on a 39-yard field goal by Mike Mercer with 4:37 remaining. George Blanda tossed five touchdown passes for Houston, but was topped by Tom Flores's six TD passes for Oakland, four to Art Powell.

Bo Jackson

THE ONLY PLAYER in NFL history with two rushing touchdowns of 90 yards or more.

Bo Jackson ran for 91 yards and a touchdown on Monday night, November 30, 1987, at Seattle as the Los Angeles Raiders thrashed the Seahawks 37–14. In all, Jackson had 221 yards rushing in only 18 attempts. On November 5, 1989, at Memorial Coliseum against the Cincinnati Bengals, he scored on a 90-yard run in a 28–7 Raider win. Jackson is also the only athlete to be named to a major league baseball All-Star team and football's Pro Bowl. He played in the All-Star Game in 1989, and was named to the AFC Pro Bowl squad following the 1990 season, but could not play due to injury.

Billy Johnson

THE ONLY PLAYER with more than 3,100 career yards returning punts.

During his career, Billy "White Shoes" Johnson returned 282 punts, also an all-time record, for 3,317 yards and six touchdowns. He played for the Houston Oilers (1974–80), Atlanta Falcons (1982–87), and Washington Redskins (1988).

Charley Johnson

THE ONLY QUARTERBACK to throw
six touchdown passes in a losing cause.

Charley Johnson was brilliant for the St.
Louis Cardinals on November 2, 1969, with
six touchdown passes against the New Orleans Saints at Busch Memorial Stadium.
But the defense failed to hold up their end
of the bargain, and the Cardinals lost
51–42.

Harvey Johnson

THE ONLY INDIVIDUAL to coach more than 25 games in the NFL and compile a winning percentage under .100.

Harvey Johnson was the player personnel director for the Buffalo Bills in 1968 when he was brought onto the field to replace Joe Collier after the club opened with two losses. The Bills were 1-10-1 under Johnson, and the only consolation to the long season was the number-one choice in the draft, which produced O. J. Simpson. Johnson returned to the front office, but in 1971 new head coach John Rauch resigned in training camp and once again Johnson was called upon to coach. This time the Bills were 1-13. Johnson's final coaching record was 2-23-1 for a winning percentage of .096.

Homer Jones

THE ONLY PRO player with more than 200 career receptions and an average of over 22 yards a catch.

Homer Jones was always a deep threat with the New York Giants from 1964 through 1969 and the Cleveland Browns in 1970. He caught 224 passes for 4,986 yards, an average of 22.3 yards a reception, and 36 touchdowns.

Rich Karlis

THE ONLY NFL player to kick seven field goals in seven attempts in one game.

The Minnesota Vikings frequently stalled on drives in their game against the Los Angeles Rams on November 5, 1989, at the Metrodome, but Rich Karlis saved the day. He booted seven field goals in seven attempts from distances of 20, 24, 22, 25, 29, 36, and 40 yards, the last coming with eight seconds left in regulation play to tie the score 21–21. The Vikings won 23–21 with a little more than two minutes gone in overtime when Mike Merriweather blocked Dale Hatcher's punt out of the end zone. It is the only overtime safety in NFL history.

Bernie Kosar

THE ONLY QUARTERBACK to throw over 300 consecutive passes without an interception.

Bernie Kosar threw 308 passes without an interception in 1990 and 1991, breaking the old mark of 294 set by Bart Starr in 1964 and 1965. Kosar's streak ended when he was intercepted by Ben Smith of the Philadelphia Eagles on November 10, 1991, in Cleveland. To make matters worse, Kosar and the Browns blew a 23–0 lead and lost to the Eagles 32–30.

Paul Krause

THE ONLY PLAYER with more than 80 career interceptions.

Paul Krause was a ball-hawking nightmare for quarterbacks during his career, intercepting 81 passes. He played for the Washington Redskins from 1964 through 1967 and the Minnesota Vikings between 1968 and 1979.

Mike Kruczek

THE ONLY QUARTERBACK to throw more than 150 passes in his NFL career without throwing a touchdown pass.

With the Pittsburgh Steelers and Washington Redskins from 1976 through 1980, Mike Kruczek was accurate, completing 60.4 percent of his 154 passes for 1,185 yards, but he could not reach the end zone. As well as failing to throw a touchdown pass, he had five interceptions.

Curly Lambeau

THE ONLY INDIVIDUAL to coach 33 consecutive years in the NFL.

Curly Lambeau coached the Green Bay Packers from 1921 through 1949, the Chicago Cardinals in 1950 and 1951, and the Washington Redskins in 1952 and 1953. He compiled a 229-134-22 record and won league championships in 1929, 1930, 1931, 1936, 1939, and 1944.

Jack Lambert

THE ONLY PLAYER to recover three fumbles in an NFL postseason game.

Jack Lambert was magnificent throughout his 11 years as middle linebacker for the Pittsburgh Steelers from 1974 to 1984, but never better than in the AFC championship game on January 4, 1976. He stopped three drives by diving on Oakland Raider fumbles to preserve a 16–10 win and put the Steelers in the Super Bowl for the second year in a row.

Tom Landry

THE ONLY COACH to go 218 consecutive regular season games without his
team being shut out.

Tom Landry almost always found a way
to reach the end zone. In 29 seasons as
Dallas Cowboys head coach, his club was
shut out only twice in 418 regular season
games. On November 16, 1970, the Cowboys lost 38–0 to the St. Louis Cardinals at
the Cotton Bowl. That embarrassment was
not repeated again for another 218 regular
season games (248 counting postseason
play), until November 17, 1985, when the
Chicago Bears throttled Dallas 44–0 at
Texas Stadium.

Dick "Night Train" Lane

THE ONLY PRO player to intercept 14 passes in a season.

Dick Lane's record is even more remarkable because he was a rookie and earned the feat in a 12-game season. He came to the Los Angeles Rams in 1952 as a free agent, having played only one season of junior college football in Scottsbluff, Nebraska. He started immediately and played 14 seasons with the Rams, Chicago Cardinals, and Detroit Lions. His career mark of 68 interceptions is third best of all time. Lane also played occasionally on offense, and caught eight career passes for 253 yards, including a 98-yard reception in 1955 and a 75-yard reception in 1956.

Steve Largent

THE ONLY PLAYER to catch passes in more than 150 consecutive NFL games.

With the Seattle Seahawks from 1977 until his retirement in 1989, Steve Largent caught at least one pass in 177 consecutive games for a league record. At the end of the 1991 season, Largent also held the top spot in career receptions (819), touchdowns receiving (100), and yards gained on receptions (13,089).

Dan Marino

THE ONLY QUARTERBACK to throw
48 touchdown passes in a season.

In 1984, Dan Marino shattered the old
record of 36 set in 1961 by George Blanda
when he reached the end zone through the
air 48 times in leading the Miami Dolphins
to the Super Bowl. Marino proved the season wasn't a fluke by scoring 44 strikes in
1986.

Jim Marshall

THE ONLY PRO player to play in 282 consecutive games.

Jim Marshall did not miss a single game during his 20-year career, playing as a defensive end for the Cleveland Browns in 1960 and the Minnesota Vikings from 1961 through 1979. His 19 seasons with the Vikings is also a record for most seasons with one club.

Rod Martin

THE ONLY PLAYER to intercept
three passes in a Super Bowl.

Rod Martin skillfully picked off three
Philadelphia Eagles passes to set up an
Oakland Raiders touchdown and field goal
in Super Bowl XV on January 25, 1981, in
New Orleans. The Raiders won 27–10.

Ollie Matson

THE ONLY NFL player to return nine kicks for touchdowns during his career.

Ollie Matson was dangerous anytime he had his hands on the ball. In 14 seasons, from 1952 to 1966, with the Chicago Cardinals, Los Angeles Rams, Detroit Lions, and Philadelphia Eagles, he scored 40 times rushing the football, 23 receiving, 6 on kickoff returns, and 3 on punt returns.

James Mayberry

THE ONLY PLAYER to score a touchdown in overtime on a pass thrown by a punter.

The score was 34–34 with just over eight minutes elapsed in overtime in a game between the Atlanta Falcons and New Orleans Saints on September 2, 1979, when James Mayberry scored. A punt snap sailed four feet over the head of the Saints' Russell Erxleben and rolled to the goal line. Erxleben attempted to pass the ball with two hands to avoid a safety, but it fell into the hands of Mayberry at the six-yard line. The resulting TD gave the Falcons a 40–34 win. For Mayberry, normally a running back playing on special teams, it was his first NFL game and the only interception of his career.

Max McGee

THE ONLY PLAYER to gain over 100 yards receiving in a Super Bowl, after gaining fewer than 100 yards during the regular season.

Max McGee was the surprise star of the first Super Bowl on January 15, 1967, at Memorial Coliseum in Los Angeles. During the regular season for the Green Bay Packers, he caught only four passes for 91 yards as a wide receiver, but in the Super Bowl against the Kansas City Chiefs, he hauled in seven catches for 138 yards and a pair of touchdowns in the 35–10 victory. A year later, in the second Super Bowl against the Oakland Raiders, McGee caught a 35-yard pass from Bart Starr, after a season of three catches for 33 yards.

John McKay

THE ONLY NFL coach to lose 26 games in a row.

John McKay knew it would be tough when he took over as coach of the expansion Tampa Bay Buccaneers, but he did not know how tough. The Bucs lost their first 26 games, starting with a 0–14 record in 1976, and had 12 straight defeats at the start of 1977. The team was particularly dismal on offense, with just 178 points in the 26 defeats, 12 of which were shutouts. In the first six home games in 1977, Tampa Bay scored exactly three points. Tampa Bay finally won on December 11, 1977, by a 33–14 score over the Saints in New Orleans.

Ron Meyer

THE ONLY NFL coach to win a game by using a snow sweeper to clear a path for his field goal kicker.

Ron Meyer's New England Patriots were tied 0–0 with the Miami Dolphins in snowy Foxboro, Massachusetts, on December 12, 1982, when he called on John Smith to try a 33-yard field goal with 45 seconds remaining. Throughout the game, a convicted burglar on a work release from Norfolk Correctional Institute, had been clearing snow off the field so that the yard lines were visible. Before Smith lined up to kick, Meyer waved the snow sweeper onto the field to clear the spot where the holder was to place the ball. The kick was good, and the Patriots won, 3–0.

Bobby Mitchell

THE ONLY NFL player to gain over 200 yards rushing in a game on fewer than 15 carries.

The Washington Redskins figured the only way to beat the Cleveland Browns on November 15, 1959, would be to stop the great Jim Brown. They were successful, holding him to 39 yards, but did not know how to stop Bobby Mitchell, who rushed for 205 yards on 14 attempts. Mitchell scored on touchdown runs of 90, 5, and 24 yards in the 31–17 win in Washington.

Art Monk

THE ONLY PLAYER to catch 100 passes in an NFL season.

Art Monk found the seams and openings in enemy defenses often enough in 1984 to catch a record 106 passes for 1,372 yards for the Washington Redskins. At the end of the 1991 campaign, Monk had 801 career receptions, just 18 shy of the all-time record.

Joe Montana

THE ONLY PLAYER to earn Most Valuable Player honors in a Super Bowl three times.

Joe Montana led the San Francisco 49ers to four Super Bowl victories and came away with the Most Valuable Player Trophy in three of them. The first was Super Bowl XVI in 1982 against Cincinnati and was followed with encores in 1985 against Miami and 1990 versus Denver. In Super Bowl competition, Montana has an amazing 83 of 122 in passing attempts, for 68 percent completions, with 1,142 yards gained and 11 touchdowns.

Lenny Moore

THE ONLY PRO player to score touchdowns in 18 consecutive games.

Lenny Moore's streak began with 3 games in 1963, extended through the entire 14-game schedule in 1964, and culminated with a one-yard run in the first game of 1965 while playing for the Baltimore Colts. An all-around performer as a halfback and flanker, Moore scored 24 touchdowns during the streak, including 19 on runs, 4 on pass receptions from Johnny Unitas, and 1 on a fumble recovery in the end zone. Three of the pass receptions went for 74, 70, and 52 yards. Moore scored 113 touchdowns during his career, fourth highest of all time.

Mercury Morris

THE ONLY PLAYER to return a kick-off 105 yards for a touchdown in his first pro game.

Mercury Morris debuted with the Miami Dolphins on September 14, 1969, and in the first quarter returned a Cincinnati Bengals kickoff 105 yards for a touchdown to tie the score 7–7. The Dolphins lost the game, however, 27–21 at Nippert Stadium in Cincinnati.

Greasy Neale

THE ONLY COACH whose club was outscored by 49 points in one half.

Greasy Neale's Philadelphia Eagles were 2-6-1 on November 30, 1941, when they were scheduled to play a home game against the powerful 8-1-0 Chicago Bears. The Eagles delighted the crowd at Shibe Park in the first half with a 14–0 lead and appeared headed for an upset. In the second half, however, the Bears scored 21 points in the third quarter and 28 in the fourth to win 49–14. Neale is also the only coach to fashion defensive shutouts in consecutive years in the NFL championship game, as the Eagles won it all in 1948 and 1949.

Al Nelson

THE ONLY PLAYER to return two missed field goals 100 yards or more for a touchdown.

With the move of the goalpost from the front line of the end zone to the rear in 1974 and the increased leg strength of NFL kickers, the return of a missed field goal is a lost art. There have been only three in NFL history of 100 yards or more, and Al Nelson has two of them, both while playing for the Philadelphia Eagles. The first came on December 11, 1966, and went for 100 yards in a 33–21 win over the Cleveland Browns. The second, on September 26, 1971, covered 101 yards and was the only Philly score in a 42–7 defeat to the Dallas Cowboys.

Ernie Nevers

THE ONLY NFL player to score 40 points in a game.

Ernie Nevers's spectacular feat came on Thanksgiving Day in 1929 as he provided all of the scoring with six touchdowns and four PATs as the Chicago Cardinals defeated their crosstown rival Bears 40–6. Just four days earlier, Nevers had accounted for the Cardinal points with three touchdowns and a PAT in a 19–0 triumph over the Dayton Triangles.

Dick Nolan

THE ONLY NFL coach to lose a 15-point fourth-quarter lead in a postseason game.

Dick Nolan's San Francisco 49ers led the Dallas Cowboys 28–13 at Candlestick Park with nine minutes to go in the divisional playoff game on December 23, 1972. But Roger Staubach rallied his team with a field goal to pull to 28–16, then hit on a 20-yard touchdown pass to Billy Parks and a 10-yard scoring strike to Ron Sellers in a 38-second span during the final two minutes of the game to win in a miracle finish 30–28.

Jerry Norton

THE ONLY NFL player to intercept four passes in a game twice in a career.

There have been 16 players in NFL history to intercept four passes in a game, but Jerry Norton is the only one to turn the trick twice, both while playing for the St. Louis Cardinals. The first came on November 20, 1960, in a 26–14 win over the Redskins in Washington. The second was on November 26, 1961, but the Cardinals lost 30–27 to the Steelers in Pittsburgh. Norton also led the NFL in punting in 1960, and his career average of 43.8 yards a boot is sixth best of all time.

Davey O'Brien

THE ONLY NFL quarterback to throw 60 passes in a game without an interception.

A Heisman Trophy winner at Texas Christian University in 1938, Davey O'Brien was a first-round draft choice of the Philadelphia Eagles a year later, and was immediately installed as the starting quarterback despite standing five feet, seven inches, and weighing in at 150 pounds. On December 1, 1940, O'Brien completed 33 of 60 passes without an interception in a passing duel with Washington's Sammy Baugh. The 60 attempts without an interception is still a record, but the Redskins won the game 13–6. The game proved to be O'Brien's last, as he retired to join the FBI.

Jim O'Brien

THE ONLY PLAYER to kick a game-ending, game-winning field goal in a Super Bowl.

Super Bowl V on January 17, 1971, between the Baltimore Colts and Dallas Cowboys at the Orange Bowl in Miami, was the only Super Bowl in which the winning score came on the final play. With five seconds remaining and the score tied, Jim O'Brien lined up for a 32-yard field goal and split the uprights as the clock wound down to zero to give the Colts a 16–13 win.

Steve O'Neal

THE ONLY PLAYER to kick a 98-yard punt.

The longest punt in NFL history was also the most perfect. On September 21, 1969, Steve O'Neal and the New York Jets were backed up on their own one-yard line against the Broncos in Denver. O'Neal's boot sailed over the head of return man Billy Thompson, hit at the Denver 30, and rolled dead at the opposite one-yard line. Denver still found its way out of the jam, however, and defeated the favored Jets 21–19.

Steve Owen

THE ONLY COACH to win an NFL championship game with the team wearing sneakers borrowed at halftime.

Steve Owen's New York Giants, who were 8-5 in 1934, met the 13-0 Chicago Bears in the NFL championship game played on a bitterly cold day at the Polo Grounds. On the morning of the game, one of the Giants players suggested wearing sneakers on the icy field for better traction, and clubhouse assistant Abe Cohen was dispatched to Manhattan College to borrow the shoes from the school's basketball team. Cohen arrived back at the Polo Grounds at halftime with the Giants trailing 10–3. In the second half, the improved footing resulted in 27 unanswered points and a 30–13 New York win.

Ace Parker

THE ONLY MEMBER of Pro Football's Hall of Fame to hit a home run in his first at bat in major league baseball.

Ace Parker made his major league baseball debut on April 30, 1937, with the Philadelphia Athletics and hit a pinch-hit home run in his initial at bat. By the end of his rookie season, however, Parker had only two homers and a .117 batting average. That fall, he played in the NFL with the Brooklyn Dodgers as a halfback and quarterback, and after performing in 56 more games with the Athletics in 1938, he stuck to football and played until 1946 with the Dodgers and the Boston Yanks. In 1972, Parker was selected to the Pro Football Hall of Fame.

Walter Payton

THE ONLY PLAYER to rush for more than 13,000 yards in a pro career.

Walter Payton is far and away pro football's all-time leading ground-gainer, with 16,726 yards in a playing career with the Chicago Bears from 1975 through 1987. At the end of the 1991 season, Tony Dorsett was a distant second at 12,739. Payton is also the record holder for most touchdowns rushing with 110, most seasons over 1,000 yards with 10, and most yards rushing in a game at 275. The single game mark was set on November 20, 1977, on 40 carries, as Payton scored the only Chicago touchdown on a one-yard plunge in a 10–7 win over the Minnesota Vikings at Soldier Field.

Preston Pearson

THE ONLY PLAYER to play in five
Super Bowls on three different clubs.

Preston Pearson moved often in his 14-
year NFL career, but still found his way
into pro football's ultimate game. He played
in Super Bowl III in 1969 with the Baltimore Colts, again in 1975 as a member of
the Pittsburgh Steelers, and in 1976, 1978,
and 1979 as a Dallas Cowboy, twice playing (and losing) to his Steeler teammates.
Pearson played on two winners and three
losers.

Vernon Perry

THE ONLY PLAYER to intercept four
passes in an NFL postseason game.

Vernon Perry had intercepted only three
passes from his safety position with the
Houston Oilers during his rookie season in
1979, but in the divisional playoff game on
December 29, 1979, against the Chargers
in San Diego, he picked off four Dan Fouts
throws. He also blocked a field goal attempt
and carried it 57 yards to set up a Houston
field goal. The Oilers won 17–14 even
though quarterback Dan Pastorini, running back Earl Campbell, and wide receiver
Ken Burrough did not play because of
injuries.

Greg Pruitt

THE ONLY PLAYER to gain over 2,000 yards rushing, receiving, kick returning, and punt returning in an NFL career.

With the Cleveland Browns from 1973 to 1981 and the Los Angeles Raiders between 1982 and 1984, Greg Pruitt totaled 5,672 yards rushing, 3,069 receiving, 2,007 punt returning, and 2,514 kickoff returning. In all, he scored 47 touchdowns.

Mike Quick

THE ONLY PLAYER to score on a 99-yard pass play in overtime.

The Philadelphia Eagles jumped out to a 17–0 lead over the Atlanta Falcons on November 10, 1985, but the Falcons scored 17 unanswered points in the fourth quarter to tie. In the second minute of overtime, a 62-yard punt by Atlanta pinned the Eagles on their own one-yard line. Two plays later, quarterback Ron Jaworski dropped into the end zone and hit Mike Quick with a pass. After outracing the Falcon defense to score, Quick and the Eagles sent home a delirious Veterans Stadium crowd with a 23–17 win.

John Rauch

THE ONLY COACH to win a game
preempted by Heidi.

The contest between John Rauch's
Raiders and the New York Jets in Oakland
on November 17, 1968, will be forever
known as "The Heidi Game." The Raiders
had the ball on their own 22-yard line with
61 seconds remaining and were trailing
32–29 in a thrilling seesaw battle. However,
viewers around the country tuned to NBC
saw not the frantic final one minute and
one second, but the movie *Heidi,* due to a
production mix-up in New York. Two plays
later, Daryle Lamonica hit Charlie Smith
with a 43-yard touchdown pass, and on
the ensuing kickoff, Preston Ridlehuber
took a Jet fumble into the end zone. The
Raiders won 43–32.

Bert Rechichar

THE ONLY PRO player to kick a 56-yard field goal in his first attempt.

Bert Rechichar debuted in the NFL on September 27, 1953, for the Baltimore Colts against the Chicago Bears, in what was also the first game of the modern Colt franchise. In the second period, Rechichar ran back an interception 35 yards for a touchdown to tie the score 7–7. On the last play of the first half, he was called upon by coach Keith Molesworth to try a 56-yard field goal. He split the uprights to put Baltimore ahead 10–7 and set an NFL record for the longest successful field goal, which stood for 17 years. The Colts went on to win 13–9.

Jerry Rice

THE ONLY NFL player to catch 22 touchdown passes in a season.

Only a strike by the players stopped Jerry Rice in 1987. He caught 65 passes for 1,078 yards and 22 TDs, despite playing in just 12 games due to the work stoppage. Rice also holds the record for most consecutive games scoring touchdowns via pass receptions, with 13 over the 1986 and 1987 seasons.

John Riggins

THE ONLY NFL player to score 24 touchdowns in a season.

John Riggins was an unstoppable workhorse for the Washington Redskins in 1983. He ran 375 times for 1,347 yards and scored 24 touchdowns during the regular season. In three postseason clashes, Riggins added six more scoring rushes.

Cal Rossi

THE ONLY PLAYER drafted by an NFL club in the first round two years in a row.

Cal Rossi was selected number one by the Washington Redskins in 1946 as a halfback out of UCLA but, to the Redskins' embarrassment, still had a year of college eligibility remaining. The Redskins tried again in 1947, picking Rossi as their first choice for the second year in a row. This time, Rossi decided against playing pro football.

Lou Saban

THE ONLY COACH whose club was held to minus 53 yards passing in a game.

Lou Saban's Denver Broncos were hopeless through the air against the Raiders in Oakland on September 10, 1967. His club had minus 53 yards passing and minus 5 yards total offense, resulting in a 51–0 loss.

Gale Sayers

THE ONLY NFL rookie to score 22 touchdowns in a season.

Gale Sayers stunned the NFL in 1965 with the Chicago Bears by scoring 14 times rushing, 6 pass receiving, once on a kickoff return, and once on a punt return. The capper came on December 12, when he scored six touchdowns against the San Francisco 49ers at Wrigley Field. First, he took a screen pass from Rudy Bukich and went 80 yards for a TD, and followed with scoring runs of 21, 7, 50, and 1 yards. The finale was an 85-yard punt return. Sayers is also the NFL's all-time kickoff return leader with a career average of 30.6 yards and six touchdowns.

Joe Schmidt

THE ONLY COACH to lose an NFL postseason game even though his defense allowed only five points.

In a bitterly fought divisional playoff game on December 26, 1970, Joe Schmidt's Detroit Lions lost 5–0 to the Dallas Cowboys at the Cotton Bowl. Dallas scored on a first-quarter field goal and a fourth-quarter safety.

George Seifert

THE ONLY NFL coach to win more than 11 consecutive road games.

George Seifert took over as head coach of the San Francisco 49ers in 1989, succeeding the legendary Bill Walsh, and won the first 16 road games of his coaching career. (In all, the 49ers won a record 18 straight road contests, including the final 2 of Walsh's tenure.) In his first two seasons as San Francisco's head man, Seifert composed a regular season record of 28-4, and was 4-1 in postseason with a 55–10 trouncing of Denver in Super Bowl XXIV.

Allie Sherman

THE ONLY COACH whose club gave
up 72 points in a regular season game.

On November 27, 1966, Allie Sherman's
New York Giants and the Washington Redskins participated in the highest scoring
game in NFL history at D.C. Stadium. The
Redskins won it 72–41, and oddities were
abundant. A. D. Whitfield, Washington's
leading rusher in 1966, scored three touchdowns, the only three he scored all year.
Defensive back Brig Owens scored on a
62-yard fumble recovery and a 60-yard
pass interception. And Redskin coach Otto
Graham called on Charlie Gogolak to kick
a 29-yard field goal with three seconds remaining to break the old scoring record of
70 set by the Los Angeles Rams in 1950.

Don Shula

THE ONLY NFL coach to go an entire year, including postseason, unbeaten and untied.

Don Shula's Miami Dolphins breezed
through the regular season with a 14-0
record in 1972, then won all three postseason games to cap a perfect 17-0 season.
The finale was a 14–7 win over the Washington Redskins in Super Bowl VII.

O. J. Simpson

THE ONLY PLAYER to gain 273 yards rushing in a losing cause.

O. J. Simpson was one of the greatest runners of all time, gaining 11,236 yards in an 11-year career in the NFL, but he never played on a championship team, not even a division champ, and he never played on the winning side of a playoff game. November 25, 1976, was typical of his career. In front of a national television audience on Thanksgiving Day, Simpson gained 273 yards on 29 carries and scored two touchdowns, but the Buffalo Bills lost 27–14 to the Lions in Detroit.

Ron Smith

THE ONLY PLAYER to gain more than 7,200 yards returning punts and kickoffs in a career.

The much-traveled Ron Smith is the NFL's all-time leader in kickoff return yardage with 6,922 and in yards gained in kickoffs and punts returned combined at 8,710. Smith played for the Chicago Bears (1965), Atlanta Falcons (1966–67), Los Angeles Rams (1968–69), the Bears again (1970–72), San Diego Chargers (1973), and Oakland Raiders (1974).

Timmy Smith

THE ONLY PLAYER to rush for over 200 yards in a Super Bowl.

Timmy Smith was a huge surprise for the Redskins in Super Bowl XXII on January 31, 1988, in Washington's 42–10 annihilation of the Denver Broncos in San Diego. During the regular season, he gained only 126 yards rushing. He added 138 more in two playoff games, then exploded for 204 in 22 carries in the Super Bowl. Slated for a feature role in 1988, Smith reported overweight and gained only 470 yards during the year with an abysmal 3.0 average per attempt.

Hank Soar

THE ONLY INDIVIDUAL to play in the NFL, coach in the NBA, and umpire in major league baseball.

Multifaceted athlete Hank Soar played for the New York Giants from 1937 through 1946, coached in the NBA for the Providence Steamrollers in 1947–48 (to a 2-17 record), and umpired in the American League from 1950 to 1973. He played in four NFL championship games and umpired in three World Series.

Gene Stallings

THE ONLY NFL coach to overcome a 25-point fourth-quarter deficit to win.

Gene Stallings and the Cardinals trailed the Tampa Bay Buccaneers 28-3 with 12:42 to play before only 22,449 spectators in St. Louis, most of whom had left for the exits. The few who stayed for the rest of this November 8, 1987 game witnessed an incredible comeback. The rally started when the Cardinals converted a fourth-and-one at the Tampa Bay 43-yard line, and on the next play, Neil Lomax connected with Robert Awalt for a touchdown. Niko Noga returned a fumble 24 yards for a score to make it 28–17. On the next two St. Louis possessions, Lomax hit J. T. Smith with TD passes of 11 and 17 yards to win 31–28.

John Stallworth

THE ONLY PLAYER with two receptions of more than 70 yards in Super
Bowl competition.

John Stallworth caught a 75-yard touchdown pass from Terry Bradshaw in Super
Bowl XIII on January 21, 1979, to bring
the Pittsburgh Steelers to a second-quarter
14–14 tie score against the Dallas Cowboys. Pittsburgh went on to win 35–31. The
Bradshaw-to-Stallworth connection clicked
again in the big game a year later, on January 20, for 73 yards. This one gave the
Steelers a 24–19 fourth-quarter lead over
the Los Angeles Rams en route to a 31–19
victory.

Jan Stenerud

THE ONLY PLAYER to kick more than 350 field goals in his career.

Jan Stenerud came to the United States from his native Norway to ski for Montana State University, and doubled as a field goal kicker for the football team. Playing for the Kansas City Chiefs (1967–79), Green Bay Packers (1980–83), and Minnesota Vikings (1984–85), Stenerud booted a record 373 field goals. He was the first pure kicker to be elected to the Pro Football Hall of Fame.

Pete Stoyanovich

THE ONLY PLAYER to kick a 58-yard field goal in NFL postseason play.

Playing for the Miami Dolphins, Pete Stoyanovich kicked a 58-yard field goal in the second quarter of the wild-card playoff game against the Kansas City Chiefs on January 5, 1991, at Joe Robbie Stadium. That was the only Miami score through three quarters, as the Dolphins trailed 16–3. Stoyanovich's long kick kept his team in the hunt, however, as Dan Marino directed two fourth-quarter touchdown drives to win 17–16.

Hank Stram

THE ONLY NFL coach to lose an 82-minute game.

The playoff battle between Hank Stram's Chiefs and the Miami Dolphins on Christmas Day, 1971, in Kansas City produced the longest game in league history. It lasted 82 minutes and 40 seconds, ending midway through the second overtime when Miami's Garo Yepremian booted a 37-yard field goal to give the Dolphins a 27–24 win. Jan Stenerud missed a 31-yard field goal in the final minute of regulation play which would have given Kansas City the win. It would be 15 years before the Chiefs played in another playoff game, 20 years before they hosted one, and 18 years before the NFL would again schedule a game on Christmas Day.

Joe Stydahar

THE ONLY NFL coach whose club scored 135 points in consecutive games.

Joe Stydahar's 1950 Los Angeles Rams were an offensive juggernaut which averaged an all-time league record of 38.8 points per game, featuring quarterbacks Norm Van Brocklin and Bob Waterfield, ends Elroy "Crazy Legs" Hirsch and Tom Fears, and halfback Glenn Davis. On October 22, 1950, in Los Angeles, the Rams buried the Baltimore Colts 70–27. A week later, the Rams won 65–24 over the Detroit Lions at Memorial Coliseum, a game in which the Rams exploded for 41 points in the third quarter.

Fran Tarkenton

THE ONLY NFL quarterback to throw for more than 44,000 yards in his career.

With the Minnesota Vikings from 1961 through 1966, the New York Giants between 1967 and 1971, and the Vikings again from 1972 to 1978, Fran Tarkenton accounted for 47,003 yards passing, nearly 4,000 more than runner-up Dan Fouts. Tarkenton also holds NFL career records for most touchdown passes (342), most completions (3,686), and most passing attempts (6,467).

Jack Tatum

THE ONLY PLAYER to return a fumble over 99 yards for a touchdown.

With Jack Tatum and the Oakland Raiders playing the Packers in Green Bay on September 24, 1972, running back MacArthur Lane fumbled a pitchout from quarterback Scott Hunter into the end zone. Tatum scooped it up and ran 104 yards for a score. The Raiders trailed 7–3 at the time, and went on to win 20–14.

Jim Taylor

THE ONLY PLAYER to beat Jim Brown out of an NFL rushing title.

Jim Brown played nine seasons in the NFL and won eight rushing titles, missing only in 1962 when Jim Taylor grabbed the honors. A bruising fullback, Taylor gained 1,474 yards for the Green Bay Packers that season, helping them to a 13-1 regular season record and an NFL championship. Taylor finished second to Brown in the NFL's rushing yardage stats in 1960, 1961, 1963, and 1964.

John Taylor

THE ONLY RECEIVER to catch two touchdown passes of longer than 90 yards in a single game.

With the Los Angeles Rams keying on and shutting down Jerry Rice, John Taylor fueled a San Francisco 49er comeback victory on Monday night, December 11, 1989. The 49ers trailed 17–0 in the first quarter and 27–9 with 10 minutes to go in the game, but Taylor kept them close with TD receptions of 92 and 95 yards from Joe Montana. San Francisco won 30–27, with the final tally a one-yard run by Roger Craig. In all, Taylor caught 11 passes for 286 yards.

Bob Timberlake

THE ONLY NFL player to attempt at least 15 field goals in his career and connect on less than 10 percent.

Bob Timberlake hit on only one field goal in 15 attempts with the New York Giants in 1965. He was 21-for-22 on extra points, however, so the title for worst professional kicker of all time has to go to Art Michalik of the Pittsburgh Steelers in 1955 and 1956. He was 1-for-13 on field goals and 9-for-15 on PATs.

Y. A. Tittle

THE ONLY NFL quarterback to combine over 500 yards passing and seven touchdown passes in the same game.

Y. A. Tittle completed 27 of 39 aerials for 505 yards and seven touchdown passes on October 28, 1962, in taking the New York Giants to a 49–34 win over the Washington Redskins at Yankee Stadium. The 36-year-old completed three scoring throws to Joe Walton for 4, 26, and 6 yards, two to Joe Morrison covering 22 and 2 yards, a 63-yard strike to Frank Gifford, and a 32-yard toss to Del Shofner. Shofner was Tittle's favorite receiver, hauling in 11 catches for 269 yards.

Richard Todd

THE ONLY NFL quarterback to complete 42 passes in a game.

With the New York Jets on September 21, 1980, against the San Francisco 49ers at Shea Stadium, Richard Todd completed 42 of 60 passes for 447 yards, three touchdowns, and just one interception, but the Jets lost 37–27. All three touchdown strikes and 18 of the completions came in the fourth quarter as the Jets desperately tried to rally from a 30–6 deficit. Clark Gaines caught 17 of Todd's passes, an all-time record for a running back in a game. Ken Anderson of the Cincinnati Bengals in 1982 and Phil Simms of the New York Giants in 1985 are the only two other NFL passers to complete at least 40 in a game.

Wally Triplett

THE ONLY NFL player to return kickoffs for 294 yards in a game.

The first black draft choice to play in the National Football League, Wally Triplett uncorked four amazing kickoff returns for the Detroit Lions against the Rams on October 29, 1950, in Los Angeles. He traveled 97 yards for a touchdown, and took three others for 74, 81, and 42 yards. Despite Triplett's heroics, the Lions were pasted by the Rams 65–24.

Johnny Unitas

THE ONLY PLAYER to throw touchdown passes in 47 consecutive regular season games.

Johnny Unitas's streak, which lasted from 1956 to 1960, would be 49 if two NFL championship games were counted. No one has come close to matching the great Baltimore Colt quarterback's streak, Dan Marino being a distant second at 30. Unitas threw for 102 touchdowns in the 47 regular season games, including 38 to Raymond Berry, 27 to Lenny Moore, and 25 to Jim Mutscheller. More importantly, he led the Colts to NFL championships in both 1958 and 1959.

Norm Van Brocklin

THE ONLY QUARTERBACK to throw
for 554 yards in an NFL game.

Norm Van Brocklin's mark has stood
untouched for more than 40 years. On
September 28, 1951, with the Los Angeles
Rams, Van Brocklin completed 27 of 41
passes for 554 yards and five touchdowns,
four of them to Elroy "Crazy Legs" Hirsch,
in a 54–14 thrashing of the New York
Yanks at Memorial Coliseum. Van Brocklin
also scored from the one-yard line to cap a
97-yard drive.

Fulton Walker

THE ONLY PLAYER to run a kickoff 98 yards for a touchdown in a Super Bowl.

The longest kickoff return in Super Bowl history is also the longest in NFL post-season play. Fulton Walker's Super Bowl run came for the Miami Dolphins against the Washington Redskins on January 30, 1983, in Pasadena in a 27–17 Washington win.

Bill Walsh

THE ONLY NFL coach to overcome a 28-point deficit to win a game.

When Bill Walsh and the San Francisco 49ers took the field against the New Orleans Saints on December 7, 1980, he was yet to be called a genius. In his second year as head coach, Walsh's career won-lost record was 7-22. Few Bay Area fans had anything positive to say at halftime. Although the Saints entered the game with an 0-13 record, the 49ers trailed 35-7 and were outgained 324 yards to 21. Many of the slim crowd of 37,949 left early. But, behind the passing of Joe Montana the 49ers rallied and won in overtime 38–35.

Paul Warfield

THE ONLY PRO player with more than 300 career receptions and over 20 yards a catch.

With the Cleveland Browns and Miami Dolphins from 1964 through 1977, Paul Warfield hauled in 427 catches for 8,565 yards, an average of 20.1 yards a reception. He also scored 85 touchdowns.

Byron "Whizzer" White

THE ONLY INDIVIDUAL to play in the NFL and serve on the U.S. Supreme Court.

Byron White was an All-American halfback at Colorado drafted number one in 1938 by the Pittsburgh Pirates of the NFL (who were renamed the Steelers a year later). White was paid the princely sum of $15,800, which made him the highest paid player in the league. He helped justify his salary by leading the league in rushing, but sat out the 1939 season to study at Oxford. After returning in 1940, he was sold to the Detroit Lions and again led in rushing. White played only one more year. In 1962, he was appointed an associate justice of the U.S. Supreme Court by President John F. Kennedy.

Ron Widby

THE ONLY ATHLETE to play pro basketball and play in a Super Bowl.

Ron Widby was a forward for the New Orleans Buccaneers of the American Basketball Association in 1967–68, and played as a punter in the NFL with the Dallas Cowboys and Green Bay Packers from 1968 through 1973. He was in Super Bowl V with the Cowboys.

Dave Williams

THE ONLY PLAYER to take an overtime kickoff for a touchdown.

On Thanksgiving Day in Detroit in 1980,
Dave Williams capped an amazing Chicago
Bears comeback to beat the Lions 23–17.
Chicago trailed 17–3 entering the fourth
quarter, but rallied for 14 points to tie on
drives of 86 and 94 yards. The tying score
came on a 4-yard run by quarterback Vince
Evans as time expired and on the subse-
quent extra point by Bob Thomas. The
Bears won the overtime coin flip, and
Williams took the kickoff on the five-yard
line and raced 95 yards down the left sideline for the victory in the shortest overtime
period ever, just 21 seconds.

Travis Williams

THE ONLY PLAYER to return two
kickoffs for touchdowns in one quarter.

Travis Williams took the opening kickoff
for the Green Bay Packers on November 12,
1967, against the Cleveland Browns in
Milwaukee, and ran it 87 yards for a touchdown. With the score 28–7, Williams took
another Cleveland kickoff all the way, this
time for 85 yards. The 35 Packer points in
the period is the all-time NFL record for
most points scored in the first quarter of a
game. Green Bay won 55–7.

Kellen Winslow

THE ONLY TIGHT end to catch five touchdown passes in one game.

The San Diego Chargers trailed the Raiders 21–14 in the second quarter at Oakland when Kellen Winslow went to work. He caught four touchdown passes from Dan Fouts and one from Chuck Muncie, covering 15, 29, 4, 5, and 3 yards, to lead San Diego to a 55–21 victory. In all, Winslow hauled in 13 passes for 144 yards in the game, played on November 22, 1981.

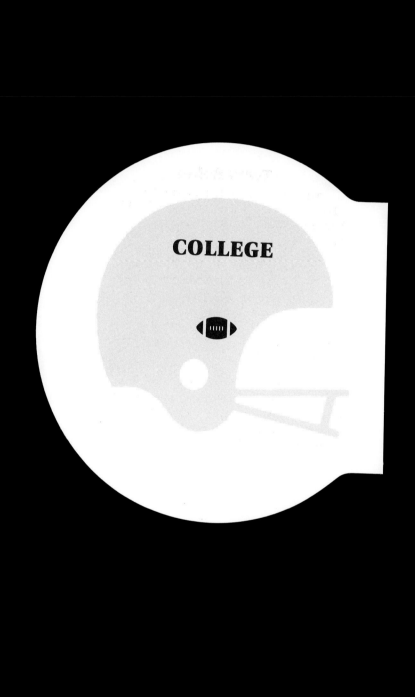

Terry Baker

THE ONLY INDIVIDUAL to win the Heisman Trophy and play in the NCAA basketball final four in the same school year.

Terry Baker won the 1962 Heisman Trophy as a quarterback for Oregon State, then starred in the Liberty Bowl with a 99-yard run to beat Villanova 6–0 on December 15. In March 1963, Baker was the starting guard for Oregon State's basketball squad at the final four, and played 27 minutes in the national semifinal, but was 0 for 9 from the field and scored no points as his club lost 80–46 to Cincinnati. He was number one overall in the NFL draft, picked by the Los Angeles Rams, but was a bust as a pro.

Red Blaik

THE ONLY COACH whose club averaged 56 points a game in one season.

Red Blaik's 1944 Army squad featuring Doc Blanchard and Glenn Davis was one of the best ever. In a 9-0 season, the gang at West Point outscored the opposition 504–35, routing North Carolina 46–0, Brown 59–7, Pittsburgh 69–7, Coast Guard 76–0, Duke 27–7, Villanova 83–0, Notre Dame 59–0, Pennsylvania 62–7, and Navy 23–7.

Bobby Bowden

THE ONLY COACH to win eight more bowl games than he has lost.

Through January 1, 1992, Bobby Bowden has a record of 11-3-1 in bowl games. For the record, he is 1-1 at West Virginia, 10-2-1 at Florida State, 9-0-1 since 1982, 2-1 in the Peach Bowl, 1-0-1 in the Florida Citrus, 0-2 in the Orange, 2-0 in the Gator, 1-0 in the All-American, 2-0 in the Fiesta, 1-0 in the Sugar, 1-0 in the Blockbuster, and 1-0 in the Cotton.

Charlie Calhoun

THE ONLY PLAYER in college history to punt 36 times in one game.

The game between Texas Tech and Centenary on November 11, 1939, at Shreveport, Louisiana, was one of the strangest, and most boring, collegiate contests in history. A driving rainstorm persisted throughout the game. Both coaches decided that it was better to punt, and hope the opposition would fumble the wet football, than to run a play from scrimmage. Texas Tech punted 39 times, including 36 by Charlie Calhoun. They ran only 12 plays, which netted minus one yard, and booted the ball away 33 times on first down. Centenary punted 38 times. The final score was Texas Tech 0, Centenary 0.

Carlos Carson

THE ONLY COLLEGE player to catch
six consecutive passes for touchdowns.

Not only does Carlos Carson hold the
record for most consecutive passes caught
for touchdowns, but they were the first six
receptions of his collegiate career. In his
debut as a sophomore at LSU on September 24, 1977, Carson caught five passes
from Steve Ensminger and David Woodley,
all for touchdowns in a 77–0 blasting of
Rice. A week later, Carson's first reception
resulted in a score in a 36–14 win over
Florida. Over the year, Carson caught 23
passes, 10 of which were TDs.

Carmen Cozza

THE ONLY COACH to have an unde-
feated, untied season spoiled in the
final minute of the last game of the season.

No game between Harvard and Yale was
more anticipated than the one at Harvard
Stadium on November 23, 1968. Both
teams went into the game 8–0. Carmen
Cozza's Yale squad led 29–13 with 42 seconds remaining, when Harvard's Frank
Champi threw a 15-yard scoring pass to
Bruce Freeman, and the Crimson scored
two to make it 29–21. After recovering the
onside kick, Harvard scored again with
four seconds left on another Champi TD
toss. Champi connected with Pete Varney
for another two-point attempt, and the
game ended in a 29–29 tie.

Anthony Davis

THE ONLY PLAYER to run back six kickoffs for touchdowns during his college career.

Anthony Davis ran back six kickoffs coast-to-coast for Southern California from 1972 to 1974, but saved his best for Notre Dame. He returned kickoffs for touchdowns covering 96 and 97 yards on December 2, 1972, as USC won 45–33 over the Irish at Memorial Coliseum in Los Angeles. On the same field against the same team November 30, 1974, Notre Dame led 24–0, when Davis returned a kickoff 100 yards and scored three other TDs as USC came back to rout Notre Dame, 55–24.

Glenn Davis

THE ONLY PLAYER to average more than eight yards per rushing attempt during his collegiate career.

Glenn Davis was known as "Mr. Outside" and Army teammate Doc Blanchard as "Mr. Inside" in 1944 and 1945 as the duo led West Point to back-to-back undefeated seasons. During his college career from 1943 through 1946, Davis rushed for 2,957 yards in 358 attempts, an average of 8.3 yards a rush, the all-time leader by anyone who carried the ball more than 300 times. On the great 1944–45 West Point teams, Davis's rushing average was an unbelievable 11.5 yards per carry, with 1,611 yards on 140 carries.

Tim Delaney

THE ONLY COLLEGE player to catch six touchdown passes in one game.

Tim Delaney ran wild for San Diego State against New Mexico State on November 15, 1969. All of the touchdowns came from the passing of Dennis Shaw, who threw for a total of nine TDs in the contest. Delaney gained 275 yards, and the touchdowns covered 2, 22, 34, 31, 30, and 9 yards. San Diego State won 70–21.

Harold "Red" Drew

THE ONLY COLLEGE coach to win a bowl game by 55 points.

The 1953 Orange Bowl looked fairly evenly matched with Harold Drew's 9th-ranked Alabama squad taking on 14th-ranked Syracuse. But in the most lopsided bowl game ever, Alabama rolled to a 61–6 win.

Bump Elliott

THE ONLY COACH to beat his brother six times.

From 1960 through 1966, the annual battle between Michigan and Illinois was brother versus brother, as Bump Elliott was at Michigan, and Pete Elliott at Illinois. Bump won the first six matchups, 8–7 in 1960, 38–6 in 1961, 14–10 in 1962, 14–8 in 1963 (Illinois's only loss of the season), 21–6 in 1964, and 23–3 in 1965. Pete finally won in 1966 by a 28–21 count.

Don Fambrough

THE ONLY COLLEGE coach to be involved in six games in one season settled by two points or less.

At the University of Kansas in 1973, Don Fambrough was involved in one nail-biter after another. He lost to Tennessee 28–27 and to Nebraska 10–9, tied Oklahoma State 10–10, and beat Iowa State 22–20, Colorado 17–15, and Missouri 14–13. The Jayhawks finished the year 7-3-1.

Don Faurot

THE ONLY COLLEGIATE coach with an 0-4 record in bowl games.

No coach has been in as many bowl games as Don Faurot without winning at least once, all while heading the football squad at the University of Missouri. He lost the 1940 Orange Bowl 21–7 to Georgia Tech, the 1942 Sugar Bowl 2–0 to Fordham, and back-to-back Gator Bowls, in 1949 and 1950, 24–23 against Clemson and 20–7 versus Maryland.

Gerald Ford

THE ONLY FUTURE U.S. president
to play in the College All-Star Game.

After a career as a center for the University of Michigan, Gerald Ford played in the College All-Star Game, which between 1934 and 1975 annually pitted a team of the best graduating seniors against the defending NFL champions. Ford played in the game on August 29, 1935, before 77,450 at Soldier Field in Chicago as the All-Stars lost to the Chicago Bears 5–0.

Red Grange

THE ONLY COLLEGE player to run for four touchdowns of 40 yards or more in the first quarter.

Red Grange may have turned in the greatest individual performance of all time for the University of Illinois against Michigan on October 18, 1924. He returned the opening kickoff 95 yards for a touchdown, then followed with TD runs from scrimmage of 67, 56, and 44 yards, all before the game was 12 minutes old. Illinois went on to win 39–14 to end Michigan's 20-game unbeaten streak.

Archie Griffin

THE ONLY COLLEGE player to win
the Heisman Trophy twice.

Archie Griffin won college football's most
coveted individual award in both 1974 and
1975 while playing at Ohio State. His con-
sistency was always evident, as he set a
still-standing record with 31 consecutive
regular season games rushing for 100
yards or more. In four seasons with the
Buckeyes, he gained 5,177 yards on 845
carries, an average of 6.1 yards per rush.

Howard Griffith

THE ONLY COLLEGIAN to score eight touchdowns in one game.

For Illinois against Southern Illinois on September 22, 1990, Howard Griffith scored on rushes of 5, 51, 7, 41, 5, 18, 5, and 3 yards in a 56–21 Fighting Illini win. Altogether, he gained 201 yards on 28 carries, in breaking the revered Illinois record of five touchdowns set by Red Grange in 1924. Ironically, Griffith had turned down a scholarship at Southern Illinois so he could walk on at Illinois.

John Heisman

THE ONLY COLLEGE coach to win a game 222–0.

The man for whom football's most famous trophy is named was coach for Georgia Tech in 1916 when his club met a hopelessly outmatched outfit from Cumberland College on October 7. Even though the third and fourth quarters were shortened by 15 minutes, Georgia Tech rolled to a 222–0 triumph, scoring touchdowns on all 32 possessions.

Bob Higgins

THE ONLY COLLEGE coach whose club held an opponent to minus 47 yards in offense in a game.

Bob Higgins's 1947 Penn State Nittany Lions had a terrifying defense that held opponents to an average of 76.8 yards per game, the best by any NCAA club since 1938. They were at their best on October 18, when they held Syracuse to minus 47 yards in offense, including minus 107 yards rushing, in a 40–0 win. Penn State finished the season 9-0-1 and allowed only 30 points.

Johnny Jackson

THE ONLY COLLEGE player to run back three interceptions for touchdowns in a single game.

Johnny Jackson picked off three University of Texas passes for Houston on November 7, 1987, and ran them back for scores covering 31, 53, and 97 yards. Houston won the free-scoring affair 60–40 at the Astrodome.

Jackie Jensen

THE ONLY ATHLETE to win consensus All-American honors in college football and the Most Valuable Player Award in major league baseball.

Jackie Jensen was an All-American fullback with the University of California in 1948, gaining 1,010 yards and scoring on a 67-yard gallop in the 1949 Rose Bowl against Northwestern. He chose baseball as a career path, however, and broke into the majors with the New York Yankees in 1950. In 1958, while with the Boston Red Sox, Jensen was the Most Valuable Player in the American League.

Howard Jones

THE ONLY COLLEGE coach with a perfect 5-0 record in bowl games.

Howard Jones coached at Southern California from 1925 to 1940, and was 5-0 in the Rose Bowl. In 1930, he beat Pittsburgh 47–14 and followed with wins in 1932 over Tulane 21–12, Pittsburgh again in 1933 by a 35–0 count, Duke in 1939 by 7–3, and a 14–0 triumph over Tennessee in 1940. The last two victories were particularly impressive, because they came over teams that had been unscored against all season.

William Kern

THE ONLY COACH whose club threw 18 passes in a game without a completion.

William Kern's West Virginia University squad holds the collegiate record for most passes thrown without a completion. The dubious mark was set with an 0-for-18 performance against Temple on October 18, 1946, in a 6–0 loss.

David Klingler

THE ONLY COLLEGE quarterback to throw 11 touchdown passes in one game.

David Klingler tossed a record 54 touchdown passes for Houston in 1990, 11 of them on November 17 to beat Eastern Washington 84–21. During his record-smashing 1990 season, Klingler also set NCAA records for most completions in a game with 48 on October 20 in a 44–17 win over SMU, and in yards passing in one game. On December 2, he was 41 of 70 for 716 yards in a 62–45 victory over Arizona State.

Joe Kuharich

THE ONLY COACH to compile a losing record while coaching at Notre
Dame.

Joe Kuharich was at Notre Dame from
1959 through 1962 and won only 17 games
while losing 23. He went 5-5, 2-8, 5-5, and
5-5 in those four years, never compiling a
winning season. Kuharich wasn't exactly
a ball of fire as a pro coach either, with a
58-82-3 mark as head of the Chicago
Cardinals (1952), Washington Redskins
(1954–58), and Philadelphia Eagles
(1964–68).

Rick Leach

THE ONLY COLLEGE player to throw for over 200 points and run for over 200 points in a college career.

Counting touchdowns and two-point conversions, Rick Leach passed for 270 points and ran for 204 in his career at the University of Michigan from 1975 through 1978.

Tommy Lewis

THE ONLY PLAYER to run off the bench to make a tackle in the Cotton Bowl.

Tommy Lewis helped give Alabama a 6–0 lead in the Cotton Bowl on New Year's Day in 1954 with a one-yard run against Rice, but watched helplessly from the bench as Rice's Dicky Moegle put his club ahead with a 79-yard TD jaunt. The next time Rice had the football, Moegle took off from his own five-yard line for another apparent touchdown. Lewis impulsively leaped off the bench and brought Moegle to the turf at the Alabama 40. The officials gave Moegle credit for a 95-yard touchdown run, and Rice went on to win 28–6. Lewis later explained his actions on the "Ed Sullivan Show."

Chuck Long

THE ONLY PLAYER to lose the Heisman Trophy balloting by only 45 points.

In 1985, Chuck Long finished second in the Heisman balloting to Bo Jackson, 1,509 points to 1,464. He had a great career as a quarterback at the University of Iowa, but it was Jackson who went on to fame and fortune. Long joined others in obscurity after finishing second in the Heisman voting.

Al Luginbill

THE ONLY COLLEGE coach whose club scored 51 points in a game, and lost.

Al Luginbill's San Diego State Aztecs lost 52–51 to Wyoming on October 6, 1990. His club also participated in the highest-scoring tie game in NCAA history on November 16, 1991, when San Diego State knotted Brigham Young 52–52.

Jay Miller

THE ONLY PLAYER to catch 22
passes in a college game.

Playing for pass-happy Brigham Young
on November 3, 1973, Jay Miller caught 22
passes from quarterbacks Gary Sheide and
Randy Litchfield for 263 yards and three
touchdowns in a 56–21 win over New Mexico at Provo, Utah.

Kevin Moen

THE ONLY COLLEGE player to score a touchdown on a kickoff after five laterals and by running over a trombone player.

With four seconds remaining in the annual grudge match between California and Stanford on November 20, 1982, Kevin Moen stood ready to receive the kickoff with his Cal team trailing 20–19. Moen took the ball at his own 43-yard line, and after five laterals, he ended up with the football again and reached the end zone. Standing in his way was a Stanford trombone player, because the band had prematurely entered the field for a postgame, and presumably, victory concert. The final score was California 25, Stanford 20.

Denny Myers

THE ONLY COACH of a team ranked
number one in the AP poll to lose a
game by 43 points.

Denny Myers's Boston College Eagles
were unbeatable through the first eight
games of 1942. They were 8-0 and had
outscored opponents by 249–19 to earn the
number-one ranking in the Associated
Press poll. All that was needed for the national title was a win in the final game on
November 28 against Holy Cross, a team
with a 4-4-1 record. Holy Cross stunned
Boston College 55–12 in the contest at
Fenway Park, the worst beating ever by a
number-one team.

Ray Nagle

THE ONLY COACH to win a college bowl game in Atlantic City, New Jersey.

The University of Utah has played in only one bowl since 1939, in the Liberty Bowl played one time only in Atlantic City, New Jersey. The game was moved from Philadelphia to the Jersey shore in 1964 and was played indoors at Convention Hall before a crowd of only 6,059. Utah defeated West Virginia 32–6. In 1965, the Liberty Bowl was moved to Memphis, Tennessee.

Bennie Oosterbaan

THE ONLY COACH whose club blocked four punts in a game, failed to make a first down, and won.

Only two teams in college football history blocked four punts in a game, and only two won without making a first down. Bennie Oosterbaan's Michigan Wolverines accomplished both on November 25, 1950, in a classic game against arch-rival Ohio State in Columbus. A raging blizzard persisted throughout the game, causing the contest to become forever known as "The Snow Bowl." Ohio State's Vic Janowicz, who won the Heisman Trophy that season, was the punter whose team went on to lose 3–9.

Jim Pilot

THE ONLY PLAYER to score on six
two-point conversions in one game.

Jim Pilot was unstoppable on November
25, 1961, in leading New Mexico State to a
54–8 win over Hardin-Simmons. He rushed
for 319 yards, the first time in history a
major college runner gained over 300 yards
in a game, and scored on six two-point
conversions in seven attempts.

John Reaves

THE ONLY PLAYER to throw five touchdown passes in his first collegiate game.

A sophomore with the University of Florida, John Reaves debuted on September 20, 1969, and hit 18 of 30 passes for 342 yards and five touchdowns in a 59–34 win over Houston at Gainesville. On the other side of the coin, Reaves became the only college passer to throw nine interceptions in a game six weeks later on November 1 in a 38–12 loss at Auburn.

Roy Riegels

THE ONLY PLAYER to run the wrong way with a fumble for 64 yards in a Rose Bowl.

Roy Riegels ran his way to immortality playing for California in the Rose Bowl on January 1, 1929, against Georgia Tech. When he picked up the loose ball, Riegels was headed in the right direction, but bounced off a tackler, spun around, and ran toward his own goal line. Teammate Benny Lom caught up with him at the California one yard line, but Georgia Tech tacklers brought "Wrong Way" Riegels to the ground. Cal tried to punt out of trouble, but the kick was blocked, and Georgia Tech had a safety and a 2–0 lead. That proved decisive, as California lost 8–7.

Jackie Robinson

THE ONLY INDIVIDUAL to score a touchdown in the College All-Star Game and hit a home run in a World Series.

After a career at UCLA where he starred in football, basketball, and baseball, Jackie Robinson played in the College All-Star Game at Soldier Field in Chicago on August 28, 1941, against the defending NFL champion Chicago Bears before a crowd of 98,203. In the fourth quarter, he caught a 46-yard touchdown pass from Charlie O'Rourke to pull the All-Stars within three points at 16–13, but the Bears pulled away and won 37–13. Robinson hit a home run in the World Series for the Brooklyn Dodgers in both 1952 and 1956.

Stacey Robinson

THE ONLY COLLEGE player to rush for 287 yards in one half.

Stacey Robinson not only set the all-time major college record for most yards rushing in one half, but did it playing quarterback. Playing for Northern Illinois against Fresno State on October 6, 1990, Robinson had 114 yards rushing in the first quarter and 173 in the second, on a total of 20 carries. He sat out most of the second half and finished with 308 yards on the ground as Northern Illinois walloped Fresno State 73–18.

Barry Sanders

THE ONLY COLLEGE player to rush
for more than 2,500 yards in a season.

In 1987, Barry Sanders was a backup
running back to Thurman Thomas at Oklahoma State. In 1988, he had the greatest
season of any college running back in history. In 11 games, he ran for 2,628 yards
on 344 attempts, an average of 7.6 yards a
carry, and scored 39 touchdowns.

Bo Schembechler

THE ONLY COACH to lose seven
more bowl games than he won.

With Miami University (Ohio) from 1963
to 1968 and at the University of Michigan
between 1969 and 1989, Bo Schembechler
rolled up an impressive 234-65-8 record for
a winning percentage of .775. But in the
bowls he was only 5-12-0, with a 1-8-0
record on January 1st. Schembechler was
1-0 in the Hall of Fame Bowl, 1-0 in the
Bluebonnet, 1-0 in the Fiesta, 2-8 in the
Rose Bowl, and 0-1 in each of the Orange,
Sugar, Holiday, and Gator Bowls.

Carl Snavely

THE ONLY COLLEGE coach whose 18-game winning streak was ended when his school gave up a win because of bad officiating.

Carl Snavely's Cornell University squad had won 18 games in a row when it faced Dartmouth in Hanover, New Hampshire, on November 16, 1940. Cornell had the ball first-and-ten on the six-yard line in the final minute trailing 3–0, and scored as time ran out to win 7–3. Trouble was, Cornell ran five plays to score because referee Red Friesell had miscalculated the downs. Since Dartmouth should have been given the ball on downs with three seconds remaining, Cornell gave up the victory in a marvelous display of sportsmanship.

Amos Alonzo Stagg

THE ONLY INDIVIDUAL to coach for 57 years.

Amos Alonzo Stagg coached collegiately at Springfield College in Massachusetts in 1890 and 1891, the University of Chicago from 1892 through 1932, and at the College of the Pacific from 1933 to 1946. He won 314, lost 199, and tied 35, and introduced a long list of innovations to football, including the huddle and the man-in-motion.

Lon Stiner

THE ONLY COACH to win a Rose Bowl played in Durham, North Carolina.

In the wake of the Japanese bombing of Pearl Harbor on December 7, 1941, the United States Army canceled all large gatherings on the West Coast, including the traditional New Year's Day Rose Bowl game in Pasadena, California, to be played in 1942 between Duke and Oregon State. Duke coach Wallace Wade offered to host the game on the Duke campus in Durham, North Carolina, and Oregon State coach Lon Stiner agreed. Oregon State proceeded to upset second-ranked and previously unbeaten Duke 20–16.

Howard Twilley

THE ONLY COLLEGE receiver to gain over 1,700 yards in a season.

For Tulsa University in 1965, Howard Twilley hauled in 134 catches for 1,779 yards and 16 touchdowns in just 10 games.

Wallace Wade

THE ONLY COACH to have an unde-feated, untied, unscored upon season ruined in the final minute of the final game of the year by a fourth-string quarterback.

Wallace Wade's Duke University Blue Devils marched through nine regular season games in 1938 without allowing a single point and earned a Rose Bowl bid against Southern California on January 2, 1939. Duke led 3–0 with 41 seconds remaining when Doyle Nave, USC's fourth-string quarterback, fired a 19-yard touch-down pass to Al Krueger. Duke lost 7-3.

Andre Ware

THE ONLY COLLEGE player to throw for 517 yards in one half.

In the first half for Houston against SMU on October 21, 1989, Andre Ware had 517 yards passing, including 340 yards and five touchdowns in the second quarter. Houston won handily, 95–21, and Ware ended the season with a Heisman Trophy.

Bud Wilkinson

THE ONLY COLLEGE coach to win 47 games in a row.

At the University of Oklahoma from 1953 through 1957, Bud Wilkinson put together the longest unbeaten, untied streak in NCAA history. The Sooners captured the national championship in 1955 and 1956. Notre Dame finally put an end to Oklahoma's winning ways on November 16, 1957, with a 7–0 upset win at Norman.